Contents

R. L. 2.9 Spache Modified Formula

ISBN: 531-09213-5
Library of Congress Catalog Card No. 83-60178

Published in 1983 by Warwick Press, 387 Park Avenue South,
New York, New York 10016
First published in 1982 by Kingfisher Books Ltd., London
Copyright © by Piper Books Ltd., 1982
Printed by Graficas Reunidas S.A., Madrid, Spain
5   4   3   2   1

ANCIENT CIVILIZATIONS

Anne Millard

Editor: Anne Priestley
Series Design: David Jefferis

A Gateway Fact Book

Warwick Press
New York/London/Toronto/Sydney
1983

Archaeology

Archaeologists study things from the past. They study fossils and bones. They study remains of ancient buildings, ships, and villages. Even broken pieces of pots or bits of clay interest an archaeologist. Two hundred years ago we knew very little about early civilizations. Historians knew something about early Greece and Rome. They knew a bit about the Near East—but not much more.

Since then, interest in the ancient world has grown. Rich people began collecting ancient objects. They wanted mostly jewels or statues or pottery. And in searching for them, they often destroyed other things. Students of the past now know that they can learn about early people from everything they find—even from a tiny speck of dust! From their ideas, and from the care they take to preserve every item, modern archaeology has been born.

River Civilizations

The first humans lived by hunting animals for food. They also ate wild grains and fruits. But they did not sow crops or raise animals.

Then, more than 10,000 years ago, some people became farmers. They settled in places like the Near and Middle East. Farmers had easier lives than hunters did. They did not have to move around to find food. They tamed animals and raised them. They grew crops. In some years they grew more food than they needed. They saved the extra crops, so they had time for new interests. Some people learned to work with clay and metal. Some learned to spin, weave, and sew clothes.

Mesopotamia

Mesopotamia lay between two rivers, the Tigris and Euphrates. The rivers flooded every summer. The farmers learned to dig canals and direct the water to where it was needed most. They grew bumper crops in the rich soil.

Extra crops were stored for food. They were also used for trade. Farmers traded some of their food for things like wood and metals, which they did not have in Mesopotamia.

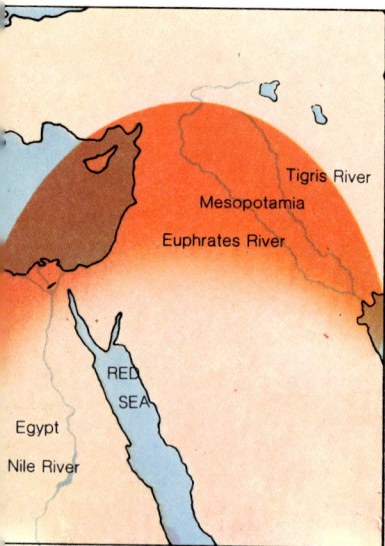

Tigris River

Mesopotamia

Euphrates River

RED SEA

Egypt

Nile River

Left: The first farmers may have settled in this part of the Near East. We call it the Fertile Crescent.

Right: The farmers raised many animals for milk, meat, and clothing.

Above: This picture is called the Royal Standard of Ur. The king is having a feast. Farmers, fishermen, and craftsmen bring gifts.

Egypt and the Nile River

Farmers in Egypt also needed river water for their crops. The Nile River flooded late every summer. The flood waters and rich mud were important for the farms. So the farmers learned to save the water for irrigation. Irrigation means watering land where there is no natural water supply. Without irrigation the crops would die during the dry times of year. Farmers in Egypt divided their land into small squares. Water flowed through ditches to reach all the crops. Everyone helped with the work.

Here is an Egyptian farm. The land is divided into squares by irrigation ditches.

Egyptian farmers grew wheat, barley, and grapes. They also raised many other fruits and vegetables.

They kept cattle, goats, sheep, pigs, and donkeys. Near the river they hunted wild birds and caught fish. The Egyptians ate many different kinds of food.

Above: This is a painting on an Egyptian tomb. You can see the people working on the land. They are plowing, planting, and gathering their crops. One man at the top is being beaten. He did not pay his taxes!

Mesopotamia

The most successful farmers in Mesopotamia lived in the southern part of the land, which was called Sumer. Archaeologists call these people Sumerians. The northern part of Mesopotamia was called Akkad. The people there were called Akkadians. These two areas became very powerful.

The Sumerian farms were well irrigated. They were rich in crops, and they could feed many people. The villages grew into towns. The towns grew to be large, rich cities.

With riches, though, came trouble for the cities. Invaders from other places wanted to steal the wealth. They wanted

Below: Most armies came on foot. But some soldiers had chariots like this one, drawn by onagers, or wild asses.

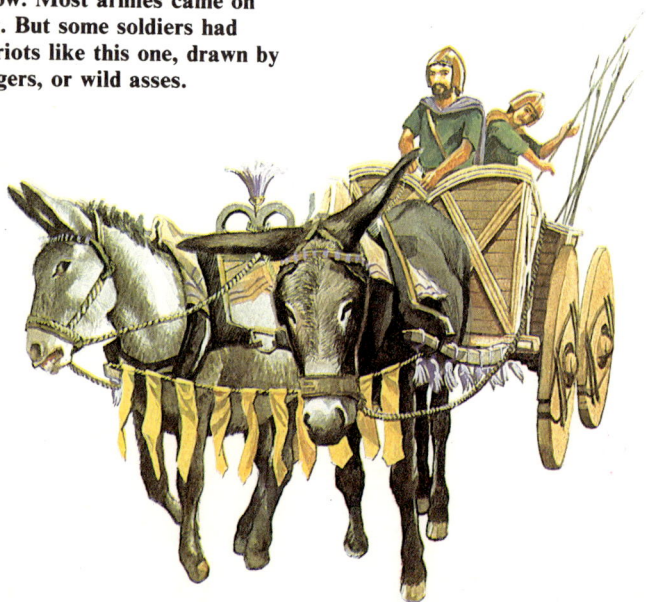

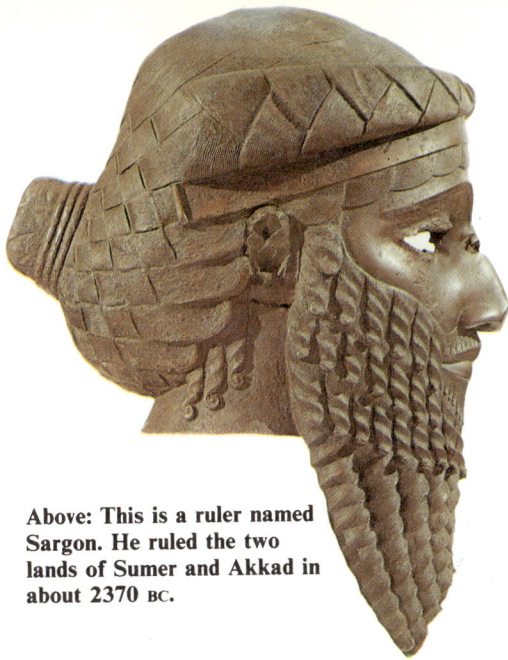

Above: This is a ruler named Sargon. He ruled the two lands of Sumer and Akkad in about 2370 BC.

Below: Hammurabi (1792–1750 BC) was another ruler of Mesopotamia. He made a code, or list, of laws. The Code of Hammurabi tells us much about daily life in Mesopotamia during his rule.

to control the fertile land.

And so, many wars and battles were fought in Mesopotamia. And the land had many, many rulers. Two of them are shown here. Sargon was an early king from Akkad. Hammurabi was one of the West Semites who gained control of Mesopotamia about 500 years later.

Princes in Mesopotamia fought against each other to control the land. Armies from other areas tried to take power. Even the Romans and the Greeks were rulers in Mesopotamia! It was a long and hard struggle for control.

Gods, Priests, and Kings

The people of Mesopotamia believed in many gods and goddesses. They believed that the gods controlled all parts of their lives. Each city had its own special god or goddess. In each city was a temple in which the god or goddess was said to live. These massive temples were called *ziggurats*. Priests and priestesses took care of the temple and its great riches. They also held religious services for the people of the city. The most important of these was the New Year festival.

Historians do not know for sure how the first kings came to power in Meospotamia. But they did rule—first the cities and then the empire. The people believed that the kings spoke for the gods, and so they cared for the kings and served them well.

This temple was built around 2000 BC in the city of Ur. The temples were once built at ground level. Later it was the custom to raise them high above the ground. They rested on tall platforms of bricks made from mud. These temples are called *ziggurats*. The ruins of many can still be seen today.

15

Left: Here is a scribe and one of his clay tablets. You can see the cuneiform script he has written. Scribes used special pens. The tips were shaped like triangles.

Below: At first, people used picture writing. Then slowly the pictures changed to simpler shapes. These were used all through Mesopotamian history.

Writing

The Sumerians had a special kind of writing. We call it *cuneiform* script. The people wrote on clay tablets. Then they baked the clay to make it hard. And so the writing has lasted for many years. We can still read many details about the daily lives of the Mesopotamians.

Scribes were the people who did the writing. They wrote all about the citizens of the city. They wrote about the temples and the kings. They told about medicine and science.

Cuneiform script is very difficult to learn. Scribes went to school to study this kind of writing.

The Next World

The Mesopotamians believed in a life after death. They believed that dead souls went to a special place, an underworld. In the underworld, there were gods and demons. It was a sad place. Life in the underworld was not as interesting as life on earth.

The Mesopotamian people thought that kings and other powerful people were treated as special even after they died. They believed, too, that good people would find rewards in the next world.

Sometimes in Mesopotamia servants chose to die with their masters or rulers.

Archaeologists found royal graves in the city of Ur. Many servants had followed their rulers into death.

Egypt

Farmers in Egypt lived in two big kingdoms. One was called Upper Egypt. It was in the south. The other, in the north, was Lower Egypt. The rulers of these kingdoms went to war. The king of Upper Egypt was the victor. He made all of Egypt into one land.

Egyptians believed the king spoke for their god, Horus. And so the king had great power. The people believed that he could do no wrong.

And when the king was a good one, Egypt was a successful land.

Egypt became wealthy from farming and trade. Egyptians also built great buildings. They made beautiful things from wood, metal, and jewels. But this was also a time of wars and trouble for Egypt.

History

Egypt has had a long and colorful history. Some people

Left: the young king Tutankh-amen, sometimes known as King Tut. He is pictured as a victo-rious conqueror. He reigned briefly during the late 14th cen-tury BC. Notice his chariot. Dur-ing the years from 1560 to 1085 BC, Egypt turned to war. Egyp-tian kings had become expert in the new skill of chariot warfare. They conquered a large empire (see below).

Egyptian Empire around 1450 BC

divide Egyptian history into "royal houses," or *dynasties*. These are rulers who came from a single family line. There have been as many as thirty-one separate dynasties in Egypt!

Historians (people who study history) have also di-vided Egypt's history into parts, or periods. You can read the names and dates of these periods in the Time Chart on pages 76 and 77.

After 1500 BC, during the New Kingdom, Egyptians made lovely jewelry and delicate carvings.

Trade

Egypt did a lot of trading with Nubia—an area of the Nile valley. (See map, page 19.) Nubia had goods from the rest of Africa—ivory, ebony, gold, and slaves. And so the Egyptians invaded Nubia and took over the land. They built towns and temples there.

Egypt had extra grain to trade—also wine, gold, and papyrus (a kind of paper). For these goods, Egypt wanted wood, silver, and copper. The Egyptians also needed horses. So they traded for them with other nearby areas. They also traded with Greece and with some of the islands in the Mediterranean.

Craftsmen

People who made goods for selling and trading were called craftsmen. Some of the craftsmen in Egypt made goods for the market. Others joined the workshops of the king, a temple, or a nobleman.

Usually a boy worked at his father's trade or craft. But he did not have to. If he was a good worker, he could try any craft or skill he chose. Even poor boys could work for the government if they were educated.

The Egyptians did not pay workers with money. They paid them with goods.

Because of archaeology, we know a great deal about Egyptian craftsmen. We can read about their work and also their holidays. We even know that sometimes they went on strike!

Below: Foreign ships sailed the Nile River bringing trade to Egypt's cities.

Life after Death

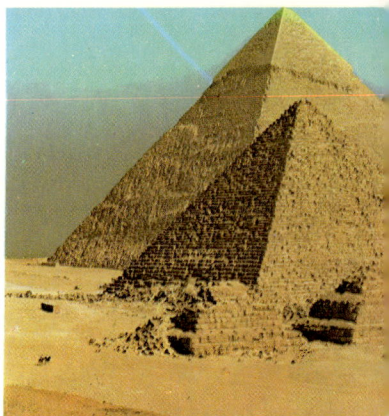

Above: The pyramids at Giza are the most famous of the Egyptian pyramids.

Like the Mesopotamians, the Egyptians believed in life after death. They built tombs to hold the bodies of the dead.

These tombs were many different sizes. Some were as small as scoops in the sand. Some were large brick buildings. Others were huge pyramids. The Egyptians spent a great deal of money on their tombs. Each one had to be supplied with everything its owner might need in the next life.

So they packed many, many goods into the tombs. They also hoped that prayer and magic would help to keep the tombs full of supplies.

But not every Egyptian could go on to a good life after death. The people believed they had to pass tests and dangers first. They had to earn a happy life after they died. And they had to lead good lives on earth. A person who had sinned on earth would be punished after death.

Above right: Here you can see inside the largest pyramid of all. It is called the Great Pyramid of Cheops.

Right: All Egyptians wanted to preserve their bodies after death. There were special ways of wrapping the body. These tasks for saving a body are called *mummification*. It took 70 days to mummify a body for the tomb. We get the word "mummy" from this practice. Many priests said special prayers for the dead at this time.

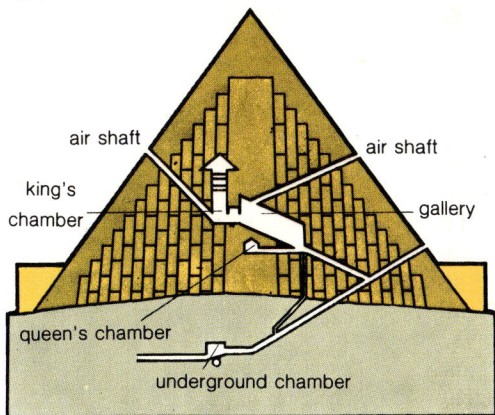

air shaft

air shaft

king's
chamber

gallery

queen's chamber

underground chamber

23

The Lives of the Gods

Religion was very important to the Egyptian people. They believed in many gods and goddesses. One was the god of the sun, Re, (pronounced "ray"). Another was the king of gods, Amun. And the people told stories about the lives of the gods.

Osiris was the god of the dead. He was killed by his evil brother. Isis and Horus, his wife and son, brought Osiris back from the dead. This story helped the people of Egypt believe life could last forever.

Temples and Priests

The temples were the homes of the gods. And so they were built to last forever. Priests took care of the temples and worked for the gods.

Behind an Egyptian temple was a courtyard. Only priests could step into the courtyards. There, in a special, very holy place, they could see a statue of the god.

The priests not only took care of the temple. They also prayed to the god of the temple and asked him questions for the people of the city.

Writing

Egyptian picture writing is called hieroglyphics. From reading this and other forms of Egyptian writing, we have learned much about their lives. We can read about their history, their learning, and their beliefs.

Right: Many gods were linked with special birds or animals. Statues showed the god with the head of this animal. That way, even people who could not read knew the name of the god right away.

Left: This head was carved from stone. It may be a god or a king from Mohenjo-Daro.

Right: Grain was kept in this big building. It was stored until needed for eating or trading. The grain was transported in oxcarts.

The Indus Valley

There were early farmers in many places, but most of the farming communities were small. In Egypt and Mesopotamia, the need to control floods led to better understanding of farming and irrigation. There, advanced civilizations grew up. The Indus Valley (in what is now Pakistan) was another successful farming area. (See map, page 28.)

A Problem
Archaeologists do not know how to read the picture writing of the Indus Valley people. So we do not know much about them. But we can see the ruins of their villages and cities. We can see their homes and palaces. One of the greatest of the Indus Valley cities is Mohenjo-Daro. It was built on very high, safe ground. Its buildings were large and strong.

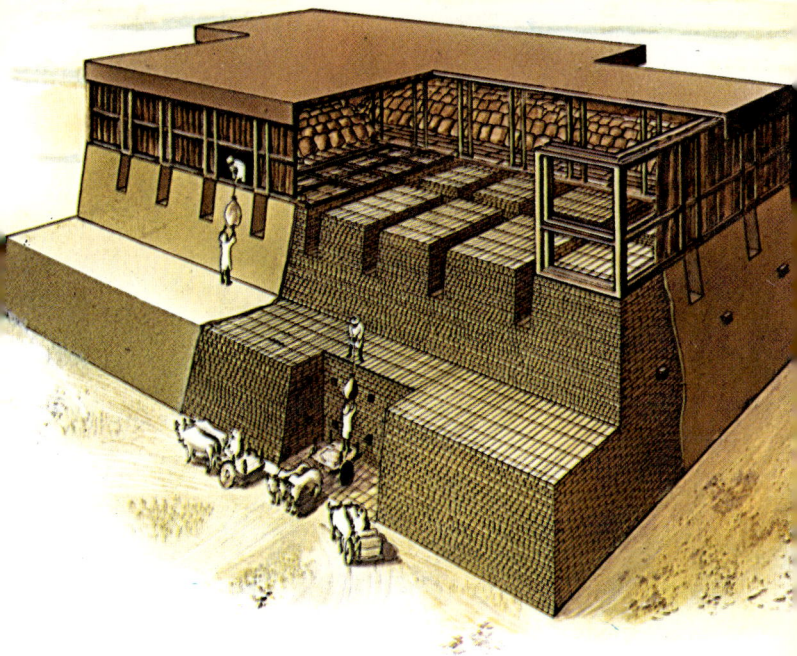

Farming and Housing

Indus Valley farmers grew wheat and barley. They also raised vegetables and rice. They were probably the first farmers to grow cotton. Cattle and buffaloes were some of their tamed animals. They even trained elephants to work for them!

Like other farmers before them, the Indus Valley settlers used mud to make bricks. They dried the bricks in the hot sun. The bricks were hard and strong for building. In some ways the city of Mohenjo-Daro seems like a modern city. The buildings were arranged in blocks. The streets were long and wide.

The houses in Mohenjo-Daro were large, with yards and flat roofs. There were staircases leading to upstairs rooms. And these houses had bathrooms and drains—just like houses today.

Around the city were strong walls and towers. The high walls made the people of the city feel safe.

Trade and Crafts

The people of the Indus Valley needed stone and metal for building and carving. To get them, they had many goods to trade. There were extra crops, fine pottery from the village craftsmen, small clay statues. Tools of copper and bronze had been crafted with care. And, from the elephants, the Indus Valley people had ivory.

They traded their fine goods with nearby lands. Some of the traders traveled the land. Others arrived by sea in huge ships.

The stone seals on the next page were carved by Indus Valley people. They used the seals to mark the things they owned. Archaeologists have even found toys made in the Indus Valley. One is a toy cart pulled by a tiny team of oxen.

The shaded area of the map shows the Indus Valley

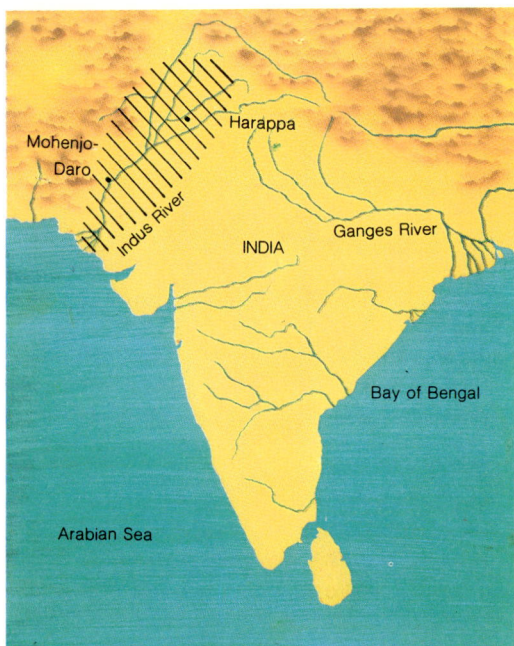

Mohenjo-Daro

Harappa

Indus River

INDIA

Ganges River

Bay of Bengal

Arabian Sea

These small carvings were used as seals, or stamps. They showed who owned the goods. And they were used to "sign" contracts. You can see some of the writing of the Indus Valley in the stone.

An Ending and a Beginning

The villages and cities of the Indus Valley did not last. Historians do not know the reason. They believe that fighting and invasions may have ended the Indus Valley culture.

At the same time, new people were moving across the area. Some settled in India, near the Indus Valley. Historians call this group the Aryans. They brought new customs and beliefs to the land. Many songs and stories about them and their gods have been saved. We can still read about them today.

More groups arrived and settled the land. Ways of life and beliefs about religion were changing with each new group of settlers. Then, around 563 BC, Prince Siddhartha Gautama was born. He founded one of the great religions of the world. He was called Buddha, meaning Enlightened One.

The Sea Kings

Not all farmers settled in river valleys. Some chose land near the sea. There were many villages and cities in the area we call Greece, on the shore of the Mediterranean. Other groups lived on islands in the middle of the sea. One of these islands is Crete.

The Mediterranean farmers grew three important crops—grain, vines, and olives. Like other farmers they also raised fruits and vegetables. And they tamed farm animals. But these people also ate fish and other foods harvested from the sea.

Crete

Archaeologists have found many beautiful palaces on the island of Crete. Even in ruins, they are wonderful to see. They have many rooms, courtyards, statues, and staircases. The walls are brightly painted. In one place, archaeologists found a throne room—and the throne was still there!

Cretan palaces were not just beautiful. They were useful, too. They were really the centers of all village life. Scribes worked in the palaces. There they made lists of the island's trade and wealth. Huge jars of oil, wine, and grain were stored in the palaces. Artists worked there, too—painting, carving, or making pottery. Archaeologists have learned much about life on Crete from studying the palaces of the island. The culture of early Crete is called Minoan after Minos, the king.

This picture shows how the palace of Knossos on the island of Crete looked when it was new.

Below: This beautiful bull is carved from stone. Things like this were often traded to other lands such as Egypt.

Above: From wall paintings we learn about daily life and fashion in Crete.

Rulers of the Seas

Later Greek stories tell about Minos, king of Crete. They say he was strong and powerful and had many ships. The stories say that he ruled the seas.

Ships were very important to the Cretans. So was the sea itself. They painted dolphins and other sea creatures on the walls of their palaces. It is easy to understand why the sea was so important to Crete. It was all around. It brought food, and it brought trade.

Writing

Archaeologists have found three kinds of writing on Crete. One is a form of picture writing. We have not yet learned to read the picture writing or the script called Linear A. But we can read

Bull-leaping. Teams of young men and women took turns leaping over the back of a charging bull. Only a part of the leaping figure survives in this statue.

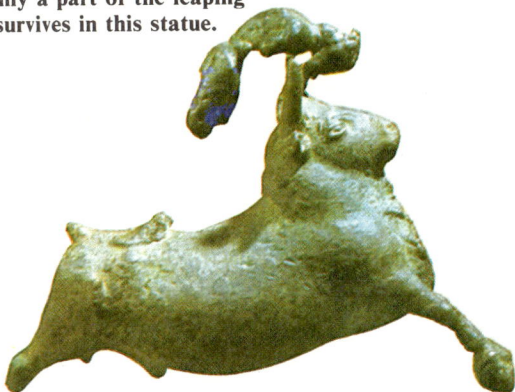

Linear B. It is an early form of Greek.

Religion

Gods and goddesses were very important to the people of Crete. But they did not build great temples on the island. Instead they had holy places. A holy place could be a cave, or it could be a hilltop. A special room in a palace could be a holy place.

The Cretans had many gods and goddesses. Archaeologists believe that the goddesses were most important in everyday life.

In many paintings, we can see people jumping over bulls. It may have been fun to watch. But it was dangerous! This sport may have been played to please the gods.

Legends

Many things happened on that small island. There were terrible earthquakes. Volcanoes harmed the villages and killed many people. And invaders from other lands attacked the cities of Crete. The Minoan civilization faded, leaving stories and legends about the island. One legend tells of a creature called the Minotaur. It was half bull and half man. The king may have worn a bull mask at religious ceremonies. Perhaps that gave rise to the legend.

Mycenae

Meanwhile life was busy on the Greek mainland. New people were always arriving. They brought with them new customs, arts, and crafts. Their languages were different from the Cretan language.

These settlers learned from the people of Crete. They copied many of the Cretan ways of life. But they also had their own customs. They had their own beliefs.

Archaeologists call these people and their way of life Mycenaean. The name comes from a Greek city, Mycenae. (See map, page 36.) There were several kingdoms in Greece. But the Mycenaean king was the leader of all the other kings.

Archaeologists have learned a great deal about early people from studying the ruins of the Mycenaeans.

R Fauvo

Changing Power

For a while, Crete had great power over Mycenae. But then volcanoes and earthquakes hurt the island. Crete grew weaker. The Cretans gave up their control. And Mycenae was ready to be strong.

The Mycenaean kings built grand palaces. They were not as beautiful as those on Crete. But they were strong and tall. Lovely paintings and bright colors decorated every room.

Below: These graves were dug in circles at Mycenae. In the foreground is the top of the Lion Gate.

Below: This head was carved from ivory. It is a soldier from Mycenae. His helmet is decorated with boars' tusks.

Royal Tombs

Archaeologists have found many graves in Mycenae. The graves were dug in circles. In them are many beautiful things—fine goods buried with the dead.

Later on, the Mycenaeans built large tombs. These were for the kings and princes of the land. They were shaped like big beehives. Then they were covered with stone blocks and soil.

Trade

Most of the Mycenaeans were farmers. Like other people, they traded their extra crops. From trading, the land became wealthy. Mycenaeans traded their crops for things

Map of Greece as described in tablets of ancient writing (Linear B).

they needed from other lands. Archaeologists have learned that the Myceneans traded with many other peoples— even some quite far away.

Religion

The people of Mycenae did not build temples for their gods. They prayed in small holy places. These were called shrines.

Mycenaeans believed in several gods and goddesses. But, as in Crete, goddesses were most important.

36

The Iliad

The Iliad is a poem about the Trojan War. It is one of the most famous poems in the world. It was written by a Greek named Homer. Homer used many older stories in his poem. Some were probably about real events. One story tells of Helen of Troy. She was so beautiful that the Greeks launched 1000 ships to bring her back from Troy. Homer said this was the start of the Trojan War. True or not, it is a wonderful story.

The Fall of Mycenae

At this time the people of Mycenae began to fight with each other. No one knows why. They began to steal from one another. And the land grew weak.

A new group of people invaded Mycenae from the north. They were the Dorians. The Mycenaeans were not strong enough to defend their land. The Dorians won the war and settled in Greece. The Dark Ages in Greece had begun.

Right: This is the blade of a dagger from Mycenae. On it you can see hunters with large shields.

Trading Empires

A plateau is an area of high, flat land. It is often called a table land. Take a look at the map below. Colored in green is the Anatolian Plateau. It connects Europe and Asia. Archaeologists have found that many groups of people lived or traveled on the Anatolian Plateau.

One of these groups was the Hittites. Their kings were very strong. They fought wars with nearby lands and built a large empire. The Hittites were a danger even to Egypt!

The Hittite Empire

Black Sea

Hellespont
(Dardanelles)

Hattusas

Anatolian Plateau
(Asia Minor)

Miletus

Cyprus

Ugarit
Syria

Mediterranean Sea

Byblos

Working with Metal

Farming was not easy for the Hittites. The climate of their area was harsh. Farmers had to work hard to grow wheat, barley, and olives.

But the land was rich in copper and silver. People in other lands wanted these metals. They were happy to trade with the Hittites.

The Hittites also learned a secret way to work with iron. They made strong iron tools and other goods. They traded or sold these for very high prices.

Above: This stone lion was carved by Hittites.

Writing

Historians have learned to read Hittite writing. We now know much about the Hittites' way of life. We can also read what the Hittites wrote about other lands at this time.

The Sea Peoples

Suddenly the Hittites were attacked. The empire dis-appeared—almost overnight! Raiders known as the Sea People invaded. They came from coastal areas, the Greek islands, and across the Hellespont from Europe into Asia Minor. They did great harm everywhere they went. Only the Egyptians were able to stop them. Some Sea People settled in lands nearby.

The Assyrians

The Assyrians lived by the Tigris River. For many years the Mesopotamian regions of Sumer and Akkad controlled Assyria. About 2000 BC the Assyrians broke free. And soon they became a strong people even though their country was small. Assyrian trade became important to many lands. Assyrian towns and cities grew up on the banks of the river.

Two cities formed the center of Assyrian trade and crafts. They were Ashur, or Assur, and Nineveh. Both are on the upper reaches of the Tigris River.

Below: These slave workers were taken in war. The Assyrian king is watching them drag a large statue for his palace.

The King

The Assyrians believed in many gods. The most important of these was named Ashur. The people thought that Ashur spoke to them through the words of their king. The king was the head of the state. And he was the religious head, too. Many Assyrians became rich working for the king.

Archaeologists have found many royal writings. The king wrote to the gods. He told them about Assyrian wars. He wrote of Assyrian daily life.

The king had to be brave at all times. In war he was a skilled soldier. In times of peace, to show his bravery, the king hunted lions.

Assyria's empire grew and grew. It reached north, east, south, and west. And still the king pushed on.

For many years the armies were made up of Assyrians. But then the empire got too big. There were not enough Assyrian soldiers. So the king forced people from captured lands to join the army, too.

The Army

The Assyrian army was very strong. It was also cruel. The soldiers fought with great force. Their weapons were deadly. Their chariots were swift. And they did great harm wherever they went. Those people whom they did not kill or force into the army were taken home to Assyria as slaves. The armies invaded many lands. After a war each new land became part of Assyria. Its people joined the Assyrian empire. They had to

An Assyrian warrior and his chariot driver. In the background is a ziggurat. Notice how the style has changed from the one on pages 14 and 15.

Right: This strange box was a weapon of war. The front end was a battering ram. Soldiers used it to ram against the gates of forts and buildings. They also hid behind it. It protected them from arrows.

pay money in taxes to the king and obey his rules. If they did not, punishments were harsh.

The empire was very large. Many people were needed to help the king. Money had to be collected. Roads had to be built. Travel became easier. And messengers told the king all the news of the land.

The End of Assyria

In some ways Assyria was too big. The king had too many people to rule. And some of them wanted to be free. Fighting broke out.

One group, the Babylonians, won their freedom. In 612 BC the Assyrian capital, Nineveh, was destroyed, and the Empire came to an end.

The Phoenicians

The Phoenicians lived on the shores of the Mediterranean. They had villages on some of the islands in the sea. And they settled on rocky parts of the shore. The cities of Phoenicia were almost like forts. High stone walls kept the people safe from attack. They always kept a good supply of food. And they collected rainwater from the roofs. With plenty of food and water, the people could live for months. Phoenicians kept their cities strong, but they were not really interested in fighting. They were traders.

The land was not very good for farming. And the mountains were steep. But the forests were rich with wood—cedar, cypress, and oak. So the Phoenicians built strong wooden ships. And they went to sea.

At first, Phoenician traders sailed close to the coast. They always went ashore at night. They traded wood, fish, and pottery to seaside villages. Then slowly they learned more about the sea. They started building different kinds of boats.

They learned to tell directions by the stars. Soon the sailors were ready to cross the open water. Some liked the new lands they found, and stayed. The Phoenician empire grew.

Kings of the Sea

In their day, Phoenicians really did rule the sea. They mined copper and silver for trading. Craftsmen made fine glass and carved ivory. The farmers had plants to trade—dates and figs, almond trees, even rose bushes. With all these goods to offer, the Phoenicians got silk from China and

Phoenician trading ships sailed the Mediterranean.

spices from India. Africa traded ebony and ostrich feathers. For these, the Phoenicians gave them wine, olive oil, and perfume. Egypt traded papyrus. In fact, so much papyrus was traded to the Phoenician city, Byblos, that paper came to be called biblos. Books were known as biblia. And so the Bible, which means "the book," got its name.

Trading Colonies

In their search for sources of metal (and to increase all their trade), the Phoenicians founded colonies around the Mediterranean. Gades (Cadiz) in Spain was one of the first. The most famous of all was Carthage, a colony of Tyre. The great general Hannibal came from Carthage.

The "Purple Men"

The Phoenicians had one craft that they kept secret. They had learned to make a rich purple dye. With it they made cloth in many shades of purple. And so they became known as the "purple men."

The purple dye really came from a kind of snail. Taken from the sea in baskets, these snails were boiled. A tiny drop of color came from each snail. Thousands of snails were needed for even a little bit of dye.

Phoenician Alphabet

The Phoenicians used an alphabet of letters. It was easier to learn than all the symbols in picture writing. Soon this new way of writing spread to many of the Mediterranean lands.

Phoenicians believed in making sacrifices to their gods. Sacrifices were people or animals killed and then offered to the gods. The Bible tells about the Phoenician sacrifices of children. Archaeologists found the remains of thousands of child sacrifices in Phoenicia. Some of the children were as old as twelve. Most were less than two years old. Their bodies were burned. Then the ashes were offered to the gods.

This is a silver coin from the city of Carthage. On it you can see a figure riding an elephant. It is Hannibal, a famous general from Carthage. Carthage grew very rich, especially from its trade in metals. In the 3rd century BC, Carthage found a dangerous rival. It was the growing city of Rome. During the Punic wars (264–146 BC) Hannibal traveled across the snow-covered Alps into Rome using elephants to carry men and supplies!

Persia

Most of Persia (known today as Iran) is high, flat land. There are mountains all around. The land was invaded many times during its long history. Then around 1300 BC two tribes arrived to settle in Persia. They were the Medes and the Persians. Both groups came from lands northeast of Persia—and they came on horseback. This was new. Many armies came on foot or in chariots. None had ever come riding on horseback.

The Medes and Persians settled in all sections of Persia, building villages and cities. Most empires grow slowly, over hundreds of years. The Persian empire grew quickly, partly because of one man, Cyrus the Persian.

King Cyrus of Persia wanted to rule a great empire. In 549 BC, King Cyrus fought the Medes and won. By 526, the Persian Empire reached from the Indus to Egypt.

Satrap Rule

Look at the map on this page. You can see how huge the Persian empire was. To control his kingdom, Cyrus divided it into sections. Then he chose a ruler, or *satrap*, to take care of each section. But the king did not want the satraps to be too strong. So he also sent soldiers and tax collectors to each area. And messengers from the king made surprise visits.

PERSIAN EMPIRE about 400 BC

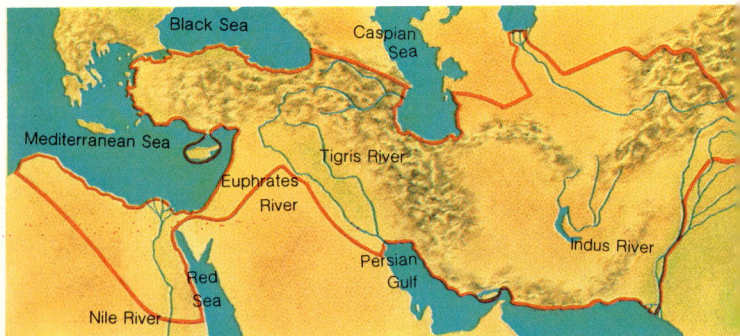

Good roads were also needed now that the empire was so big. One famous road was 1620 (2600 km) miles long. Royal messengers took over a week to travel it!

Religion

The Persians built tall towers to honor their gods. Holy fires burned there at all times. A special class of priests was called the Magi. They prayed to the gods to make life better for all their people.

The chief god was Ahura Mazda. The king was supposed to represent him on earth. But the fame of one god spread well beyond Persia. He was Mithras, the sun god. The Roman legions later adopted this god.

Right: A Persian soldier. He was one of the soldiers who guarded the king. You can see his spear and bow and arrows. His group was called the Royal Guards. There were always exactly 10,000 soldiers in the Royal Guards—so, as a group, they seemed to be immortal!

Far East and West

So far we have read about the Near East and the Mediterranean areas. In these places, the first villages and cities arose. Now we will look at other areas. Far to the east and west were different groups of people. And their ways of life are important in our study of history.

China

Many river valley farmers had settled in China. There by the Yellow River the soil was rich. Before 600 BC these early farmers used tools of wood and stone. They grew wheat, barley, and vegetables. Rice was not yet an important crop. The farmers also raised hemp, a plant they used for making

cloth. And silk for rich people's clothes came from silk-worms. Chinese farmers kept cattle, buffaloes, pigs, sheep, dogs, and horses.

The crops grew well, and so did the towns. Craftsmen were skilled at pottery and bronze work. Others carved stone and learned to work with jade, a lovely green stone. Beautiful Chinese goods were traded with other lands for horses, pearls, furs, and slaves.

About 600 BC, the Chinese learned to make strong iron tools. With iron drills they dug salt mines. They also found out how to make paper from hemp. They even had a tool to tell when an earthquake was coming!

The Son of Heaven

The early rulers of China were called emperors. Each emperor ruled the many different Chinese villages and towns as one land. The people believed that the emperor spoke for the gods. And so he was known as the Son of Heaven.

The emperors had many priests and other workers to help them rule such a huge land. One person alone would not be able to serve both the gods and the large empire of China.

Sacrifices and Burials

The Chinese believed in making sacrifices—offering people or animals to be killed in honor of the gods. Sometimes a sacrifice was made when a new building was raised. And when a ruler was buried, sacrifices were offered.

Chinese dead were buried in tombs. Wall paintings and goods inside the tomb tell us about Chinese daily life. Tiny models of the dead person's house and village have also been found.

The first examples of Chinese writing are on bones. Called "oracle bones," these were used to ask advice from the gods.

Warfare

Daily life in early China was not peaceful. Wars often broke out when rulers from different areas fought each other for land and power. Chinese soldiers traveled on foot and in horse-drawn chariots. Later the armies moved on horseback. Bows and arrows, spears, and swords were common weapons. The Chinese armies were strong and cruel.

The Great Wall of China is 1500 miles (2400 km) long. It was built in the 3rd century to keep out invaders from the north. The wall is so long it has 25,000 watchtowers!

Customs

China was a vast empire. It was far from other settled areas. So it is no surprise that the Chinese customs were quite different. The Chinese used chopsticks for eating. They used brushes for writing. And they developed ways of printing that are still used today.

Left: Here is the famous Great Wall of China. It was built on the orders of one of the Chinese emperors. He wanted to keep out invaders from the north.

Right: There was a very wise man in China named Confucius. He was born in 551 BC. He tried to bring peace and order to the land. His teaching became very important to all the Chinese people. One of his lessons was "What you do not want done to you, do not do to others."

Nomads of the Steppes

The land between the Indus River Valley and China is mostly grassland and desert. We call this area the steppes. Here an early group of people lived as nomads. Nomads are people who move from place to place with animal herds. About 900 BC, the people of the steppes gave up farming for a wandering life. Maybe their land was too dry to raise crops. And so they moved around, looking for pasture for their horses, cattle, and sheep. The men rode on horseback. The women rode in oxcarts. Their homes were huge tents made of felt.

Archaeologists learned that the nomads loved colored cloth. And they had many gold and silver objects that they hung on their horses or wore on their clothing.

The nomads lived on the milk and meat that they got from their animals. They also hunted and fished for food.

Scalps and Skulls

The Scythians were a famous and cruel group of nomads. They took scalps from their enemies and even used enemy skulls for drinking cups! They stole from villages and cities. And they made traders pay a tax to cross their lands.

A Funeral

The nomads buried their dead under great mounds of dirt. A famous Greek historian named Herodotus wrote about the funeral of a nomad chief. The dead body was preserved in wax and herbs. It was carried throughout the land. Servants and horses were then buried with the chief. And a year later, fifty more horsemen and horses were killed as sacrifices. Their bodies were placed around the grave.

Right: The Scythians were expert horsemen and skilled with bows and arrows. This bronze jar shows Scythians turning to fire arrows at the enemy behind them.

In the New World

No one knows for sure when people first came to the New World. It was probably during the Ice Age. At that time, the sea was low. There was a land bridge across the Bering Strait between Russia and Alaska. Hunters and farmers crossed this land bridge. They settled in many parts of the New World.

Mexico

Farming in the New World began in Mexico. The crops were not the same as in the Old World. Farmers here grew beans, maize (corn), and other vegetables.

Early Mexican farmers did not have cattle, sheep, and pigs. They raised turkeys and small dogs for meat. They also hunted and fished for food.

The Olmecs were an important Mexican society. They did not live in cities. But they did get together to build temples. They raised huge mounds of earth and built the temples on top.

Above: Olmec craftsmen carved large stone heads like this one with its "baby face." They also made many objects from jade.

Peru

Farming was not as important in Peru. Settlers built their homes on the coast of this land. Fish and other sea creatures were more important than farm crops. They did grow maize, though, and also vegetables and cotton.

Most of their food came from hunting, fishing, and farming. But the people of Peru also kept guinea pigs in their homes. They raised them for meat!

Llamas were trained to carry heavy goods. Their wool was made into fine clothing. Cloth from Peru was strong as well as beautiful.

MEXICO   OLMECS

MOCHICAS   PERU

Above and right: The Mochica civilization arose on the coast of what is now Peru. The Mochicas were famous for their fine pottery. Many of their pots show figures of humans. From them we can get an idea of how the people looked and what they wore.

57

Europe Awakes

While empires were built and wars were fought in the East, Northern Europe was quiet. The people of this area were farmers. They lived in small groups. Archaeologists often name these people after the places where they lived. Or they are named after an object or tool that they made. These early Europeans were skilled craftsmen, and they did fine work with metals. When they wanted to, they worked together to build great things.

The Celts

We call one group of early Europeans the Celts. They moved from their homes in Northern Europe to other areas. They traveled to Spain, Ireland, Scotland, and Italy. Everywhere they went, the Celts were warlike.

They attacked villages and towns in many lands of Europe. They even attacked Rome! And still they moved on. Some Celts traveled into Asia and settled there. They traveled far and wide, and they were many in number. But they never united to form an empire.

The Celtic tribes often fought against each other as well as other lands. They built wood forts on the tops of hills. Their weapons were made of bronze and iron. Even the Celtic priests often went with the soldiers into battle!

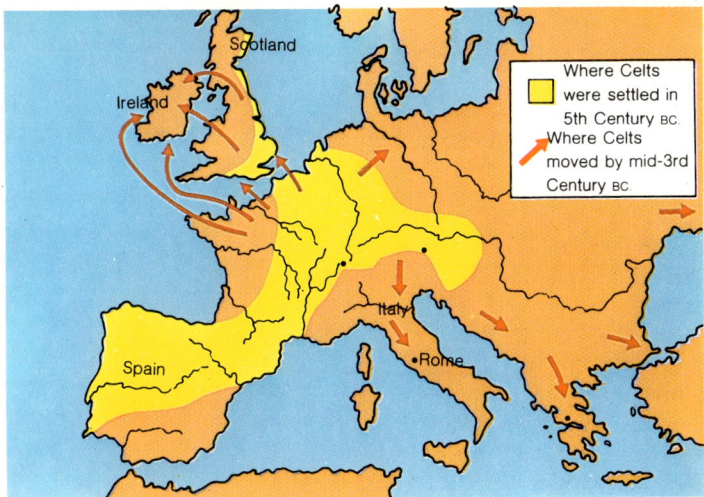

Above: This map shows how the Celts spread across Europe.

Warriors and Poets

A Roman writer left a description of the Celts. He said the Celts loved war and were quick to go to battle. They dashed into the fight in chariots, with weapons of iron and bronze.

The Celts had no form of writing, but they did pass on stories, legends, and history. Celtic poets, called bards, were famous. Their poems and songs told of Celtic heroes, soldiers, and priests. Celtic priests were called druids. They were wise men and teachers as well as priests. It took twenty years to become a druid!

Farmers and Fashions

The Celts were good farmers. They grew wheat and barley in their small fields. They used a sickle with a curving blade to reap crops. Celtic farmers kept horses, cattle, sheep, and many pigs. Their houses were made of wood or of branches coated with mud. Men wore tunics and trousers. The women wore dresses. All the Celts wore plenty of jewelry, including neck rings called torques. Some even colored their bodies with a blue dye called woad.

Life after Death

The Celts buried food and goods in the grave when someone died. Thus the dead would be ready for a life after death.

The Wine Trade

Early writers and archaeologists agree that the Celts loved wine. They imported it from Greece along with pottery and metal goods.

Left: The Battersea Shield was made of bronze by Celtic craftsmen. Beautifully decorated, this shield once had wood or leather backing. The Celts were very skilled metalworkers. They traded their armor, weapons, and jewelry to many lands, along with food, slaves, and hunting dogs.

Below: The Celts had special respect for human skulls. They even set them up in stone shrines. Celtic holy places were often groves or forests. There they built simple wooden statues for their gods. Roman writers described the Celts as harsh and cruel. Later rulers agreed. They banned druid priests and stopped all human sacrifices.

Greece

After the fall of Mycenae around 1200 BC, Greek culture entered a dark age. For a while, it seemed that all art and learning were gone. Even the skill of writing had been lost.

But then life began to improve. The Mycenaean kings were gone. Now larger towns became city-states. The most important of these were Athens, Sparta, and Thebes. They were ruled by noblemen.

The Greeks built boats and went to sea. They began to trade. From the Phoenicians they got jewelry and purple cloth—and a new, simpler alphabet. They copied parts of the Phoenician alphabet and used it for writing their own language.

Greek ships sailed all along the Mediterranean. And traders and ship owners grew rich. In the city-states, the people wanted more control. They felt that the nobles did not understand the needs of ordinary people. The noblemen had to share their power with the common people. Soon all free men could take part in government. All citizens could vote. Women, slaves, and foreigners were not counted as citizens. But free men were expected to pay taxes. And they took an active part in all aspects of government. This was the start of democracy—government by the people.

GREECE IN THE 5TH CENTURY BC

MACEDONIA

GREECE

Thermopylae

Troy

Thebes

Athens

Sparta

CRETE

Below: In each city-state, the people fought as soldiers if they were needed. But in Sparta, a strict city-state, the army was permanent. All citizens had to join the army. They were aided by slaves called helots.

Above: This is the Acropolis in Athens. It began as a Mycenaean fort. It contains some of the most beautiful buildings of classical Greece. The Greek word "acropolis" means "high city."

Above: Plays in Greece were acted in theaters like this one. All the actors were men. They wore masks to show what roles they were playing.

Classical Greece

After 500 years of the so-called Dark Ages, Greek culture flowered again. This time, from 500 to 336 BC, is known as the classical period. Art and science began to grow once again.

The city-states were small. Each citizen took part in ruling—and, of course, fighting, if necessary.

Arts and Sciences

This was a time when art in Greece was finer than any the world had ever known. Pottery, jewelry, statues, and goods of every kind were in demand from people in many lands. Styles of art and building from classical Greece are still being copied today. Scientists and thinkers studied the natural world and the people around them. In Athens the first theaters were built, and some of the finest plays of all time were written.

Trade and Religion

There were marketplaces in

Left: It is hard to believe that such beautiful pottery was used every day! Jars like this, which have been saved, are now prized for their beauty. And they are of great value to archaeologists as well.

Below: These are two of the Greek gods, Hermes and the infant Dionysus. Hermes was the messenger of the gods. Dionysus was the god of good living and wine.

the city-states for buying and selling goods. But Greece became rich by trading with other lands. Coins came into use. Athens was lucky. It owned silver mines. The Athenians could make all the silver coins they needed!

Greek gods and goddesses were said to live on Mount Olympus. Greeks built shrines to the gods in their homes and in great temples. And games, such as the famous Olympic Games, were held in honor of the gods.

Left: mosaic of Alexander the Great, based on a Greek painting.

A strong king from the north was King Philip of Macedon who ruled from 359 to 336 BC. He had a large army and plenty of gold to pay for his wars. He wanted to rule all of Greee as one land. This he did, but then he was killed. Archaeologists have found a very rich tomb. They think it may be the tomb of King Philip.

Alexander, 336–323 BC

Alexander, Philip's son, was a skilled soldier. He was also one of the greatest leaders of all time. Alexander was only twenty when he became king! He died when he was thirty-three. In thirteen years he finished the war against Persia that his father had planned. And he formed a giant empire. He ruled the Persian empire and lands to the south as far as Africa and east into India. But the empire was too huge to unite as one land. The empire broke up after Alexander died.

He is known as Alexander the Great. The map shows the size of his empire.

Alexander and After

The classical period was a great time for the Greek arts and sciences. But it was also a time of constant war. First the Persians invaded from the east. The Greek armies held them back. Then the Greeks fought one another in a civil war. And several other smaller wars followed as well.

Separate Kingdoms

Soon after Alexander died, his wife and baby son were killed. The generals from Alexander's army fought with each other. Then they chopped up Alexander's empire into several kingdoms. Each was ruled by a different general. Even Persia was lost to other warring armies. And so the empire Alexander had fought for was gone.

In the new kingdoms, Greek customs, art, and learning were very strong. Greek ideas were discussed. Greek medicine was copied. Art, writing, and building— all were in the Greek style. Alexander founded the city of Alexandria in the new kingdom of Egypt. Alexandria became a center for learning, with a library finer than any in the world.

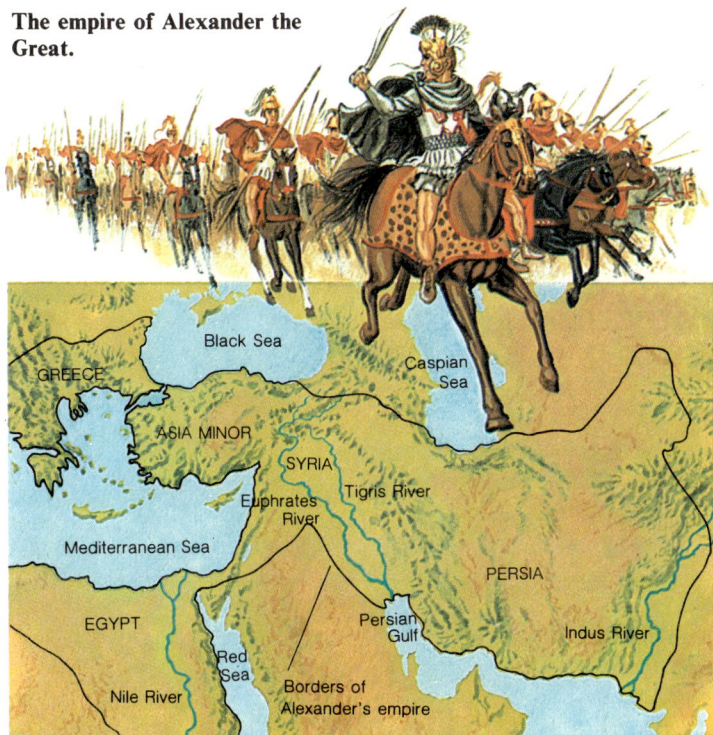

The empire of Alexander the Great.

Black Sea

GREECE

Caspian Sea

ASIA MINOR

SYRIA

Euphrates River

Tigris River

Mediterranean Sea

PERSIA

EGYPT

Persian Gulf

Indus River

Red Sea

Nile River

Borders of Alexander's empire

Rome

A famous legend tells about the founding of Rome. Twin boys, Romulus and Remus, were sons of the god of war, Mars. A wicked uncle left them in the woods to die. But a wolf found them and took care of them. In 753 BC, when the twins were grown, they founded the city of Rome.

We do not know exactly when Rome was really founded, but we do know that a hilltop people called the Etruscans ruled in Rome before the 8th century.

The Etruscans

We have not learned to read Etruscan writing. But we do know that the Etruscans did very fine work with bronze and gold. And they are famous for clay figures and tomb paintings like the one on the opposite page. Etruscans liked games, music, and racing. They brought the very first chariots to Italy.

A New Republic

The last Etruscan king of Rome was driven out about 510 BC. The Romans had come to hate the very title of king. They set up a republic in which the people would vote for their rulers. Two groups were set up to govern. One was made up of all the citizens. The other, called a senate, was made up of noblemen. They had the real power. Two consuls were elected every year to lead the government. But even with elections, there was trouble in the new republic.

An Emperor for the Empire

The empire became too big to govern easily. Different groups struggled for power. Finally there were long civil wars. The murder of Julius Caesar, a famous general and leader, took place in 44 BC. Then, in 27 BC, his nephew, Octavius, took power and became emperor. Thereafter he was known by the title of honor, Augustus.

Life in the Republic

Grain, vines, and olives were the main crops in Rome. Vegetables were also grown, as well as fruit. Roman farmers, like others before them, kept animals for work and for food. In the early days Rome had only a few craftsmen and traders. Everyone else was a farmer. Then times changed. Soon rich men owned huge estates. Hundreds of slaves worked for them. The small farmers could not compete. They had to give up their farms. The same thing happened among craftsmen and traders. Large workshops with slaves took over all the work. Finally, in Rome, those without work, food, or money were given grain to stay alive.

Citizens

Citizens in Rome had many rights and privileges. Everyone wanted to become a Roman citizen. And so, as the empire grew, people from other lands asked to be citizens. So did the ex-slaves of the city. By AD 212 Rome allowed most free men to become Roman citizens.

Many Romans lived in country houses on farms like this one. In the days of the empire, rich people also built huge palaces.

The Army

The Roman army was famous. It was well trained, and it was big. At one time, Romans served in the army only when they were not needed on their farms. Then Rome took control of all of Italy. The army marched farther into other lands. A large empire was won. Now the army was needed as never before. So the army became a full-time job.

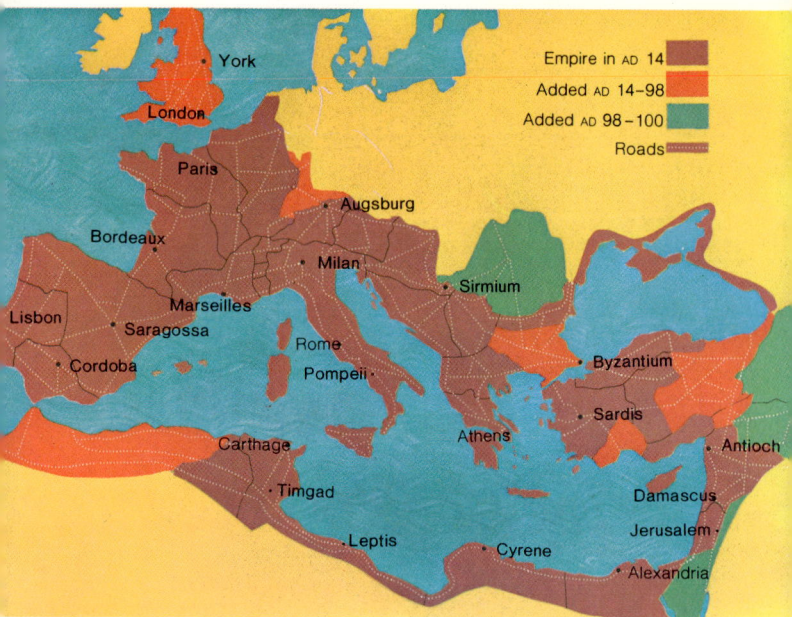

Empire in AD 14
Added AD 14–98
Added AD 98–100
Roads

York
London
Paris
Augsburg
Bordeaux
Milan
Sirmium
Marseilles
Lisbon
Saragossa
Rome
Cordoba
Pompeii
Byzantium
Carthage
Athens
Sardis
Antioch
Timgad
Damascus
Leptis
Jerusalem
Cyrene
Alexandria

The Glory of Rome

The Romans had once been happy to lead simple lives. But times were changing. The empire was growing. Goods, riches, and slaves flooded into Rome.

The rich had large houses in the city and in the country. Their homes had heat, baths, and beautiful gardens. They were waited on hand and foot by slaves. They filled their houses with luxuries and ate the finest of foods.

Slaves

It was a good life for the rich. But it was misery for many of the slaves. To be slave to a kind owner was not so bad. He might give you your freedom. But most owners were cruel, and slaves led hard, short lives.

The slaves tried many times to fight for better lives. But they always failed. And there was nowhere to run to.

Bread and Circuses

The poor of the city were given grain. And they were offered free shows and sports to watch. Chariot races called circuses were exciting to watch. But some of what went on was dreadful and cruel. Gladiators were people who fought animals or other men to the death. It was a bloody sport.

City Living

An aqueduct is an overhead pipeline for carrying water. Aqueducts were built throughout the Roman Empire. Much water went to the free public baths that were found in many towns.

Below: New materials (such as concrete), new tools, and many slaves helped the Romans build aqueducts.

Since all books were written by hand, they were very expensive. Public libraries were set up so that the people of the city could read and study.

In Roman cities most people lived in apartments. They could rent one or more rooms. Few apartments had baths, water, or places to cook. But there were the public baths. And plenty of shops sold drinks and cooked food.

Religion

Roman gods and goddesses were much like those of the Greeks. And in Rome some emperors were honored as gods. Romans allowed conquered peoples to follow their own faiths—as long as obedience and loyalty to Rome came first! Both Christians and Jews were persecuted because they put religious obedience before obedience to Rome.

The Barbarian Invasions

Many forts guarded the borders of the empire. Good roads were built so that soldiers could move in quickly wherever they were needed. But from the 3rd century on, nothing could stop the Barbarians from the north.

Left: This coin shows the Roman emperor Constantine.

Below: Some of the walls of Constantinople still stand today.

Crisis in the Empire

Barbarians settled on land near the borders. The empire was growing weaker as rulers fought among themselves. Then a powerful man seized control. His name was Diocletian. In his reign, Roman Christians were treated with cruelty. But Diocletian solved many problems of the empire. He stopped the invasions. He took care of problems among the rulers. Then he divided the empire in two—each part with its own emperor. Their heirs were given the title Caesar.

Constantinople, the New Rome

In AD 306 another strong emperor, Constantine, took charge of the whole land himself. He accepted the Christians and their religion. And he moved the capital of the empire to Constantinople.

In later years, the Roman empire split again. The Eastern Empire had a long future. But the West was again invaded by Barbarians. And Rome fell.

Below: This carving in marble shows Roman soldiers fighting Barbarian invaders. The tribes wanted to share Rome's wealth. Instead, they destroyed it.

Further Facts

Time Chart: 3500 BC–AD 500

	MIDDLE EAST	ASIA	EUROPE	THE AMERICAS
BC 3500	Irrigation in Egypt and Mesopotamia; invention of writing; cities develop in Mesopotamia; Egypt unified	Early farmers in China growing millet	Building of stone monuments and use of farming spread across Europe	Villages on coast of Peru based on fishing and plant gathering
3000				
BC	Archaic period in Egypt; cities of Sumer; Egypt's Old Kingdom; pyramids built; Royal Graves at Ur	Rise of Indus Valley people	Early Minoan culture in Crete	Farmers growing maize and cotton in Mexico and Peru
2500		Indus River / INDIA		
BC	Sargon of Akkad		Indo-Europeans move southeast into Middle East and Asia	
2000			Greek-speaking people arrive in Greece	
BC	Egypt's Middle Kingdom; Hammurabi of Babylon	Arrival of Indo-Europeans in India		First pottery and fine weaving in Peru

1500	Egypt's New Kingdom		Great palaces of Crete; rise of the Mycenaeans	
BC 1000	Hittite Empire; Rise of the Phoenicians; raids of Sea Peoples	Shang dynasty in China; development of caste system and Hindu religion in India; Chou dynasty in China	Building of Stonehenge; Crete destroyed	
BC 500	Rise of Assyria; Carthage founded; Babylonian Empire; Late Period in Egypt; Persian Empire	Iron Age in India; Great Wall of China begun; Birth of the Buddha (563); Birth of Confucius (551)	Rise of the Etruscans; Founding of Rome (753); Rise of Greek city-states	Olmecs of Mexico: platforms and pyramids; Chavin culture in Peru
BC 0	Conquests of Alexander; Conquest by Rome	The Warring States Period in China; Alexander in India; Ch'in dynasty in China; Han dynasty in China	Greek wars against Persia; spread of Celtic culture; Peloponnesian War; Alexander the Great; spread of Roman Empire	Mochica and Nazca cultures in Peru
AD 500	Birth of Jesus Christ; Constantinople new capital of the Roman Empire (330)	Gupta Empire in India; China in turmoil	Most of Europe under Roman rule; barbarians begin threatening empire; Christians no longer persecuted	

Pottery Puzzles

Wherever archaeologists dig, they look for clues to the past. Something that might not seem special to us might be very exciting to an archaeologist. One example is pottery.

Unlocking the Past

Even a small broken piece of pottery can be important. It can tell the archaeologist about the people who made it. The making of pottery began when early farmers started to settle in villages. Pots were not valuable. When pottery broke, it was thrown away. And grave robbers could not be bothered with pottery. And so a good deal has survived.

From the style of the pottery, archaeologists can tell if two villages date from the same period. If they find the same style in another place, they know the dates must be similar.

A new style of pottery among the old may tell an archaeologist that new people arrived in the village or city, bringing their things with them.

Goods that were traded were often packed in pots.

6th century AD

About 100 BC

About 700 BC

Some pots are found in one piece. Others are broken.

Pots found in houses of 1500 BC.

And so a discovery of pottery can tell historians about trade among the ancient lands.

To make fine pottery takes skill. Archaeologists study the quality of the pottery they find. And they learn even more about the skilled craftsmen of the land that they are studying.

If we could take a slice from an archaeological dig, it might look like this. Of course the oldest objects are in the lowest layer. More modern things are at the top. If any writing is found, it will be easier to date the society. But archaeologists have other ways of learning dates. They can figure the age of clay. And a way of testing clay called *thermoluminescence* even tells the age of a pot!

Signs of Civilization—Metal

One way to work with metal is the lost wax method. A model is made of wax (left). Clay or plaster is poured around it (above). This is then heated until the wax melts and runs out.

At one time historians divided the history of ancient peoples into the Stone Age, the Bronze Age, and the Iron Age. This was an easy way to look at ancient history, but it was too simple.

The discovery of one material never meant that another was no longer used. And the use of metal began at different times in different parts of the world. Some tribes are still living in a Stone Age today!

Working with Metal

Early farmers discovered that some rocks were easier to work with if they were heated. Then they could be hammered and chipped into shape. These were rocks containing

Above: Now the shape of the figure (in the plaster or clay) can be filled with hot liquid metal.

Above: When the metal is hard, the clay or plaster can be chipped away—carefully! The solid metal figure remains.

metal. Then, probably by accident, they found that gold, silver, and copper could be melted. Then they could be poured into molds. Mixing copper and tin made an even harder metal, bronze. And later a way was found to make iron, the hardest of all.

Metal for Trade

Societies that had their own metals were lucky. Those who had none traded for them. The trade brought wealth to some countries. And almost everywhere the craftsmen who worked with metals were treated with great respect.

Iron was of more value than bronze because it is much harder. When the Hittites first learned how to make iron, they kept the secret, so the price was high!

Signs of Civilization— Writing

Writing is one of the most important clues about a society. Written records tell about the history and daily lives of the ancient people. And the writing itself tells how advanced the society had become.

Below: The name Ptolemy in hieroglyphics.

Below left: The Rosetta Stone led to our understanding of Egyptian hieroglyphics. It has Egyptian writing translated into Greek.

P T O L M I S

Ornament with the name
of Tutankhamen

82

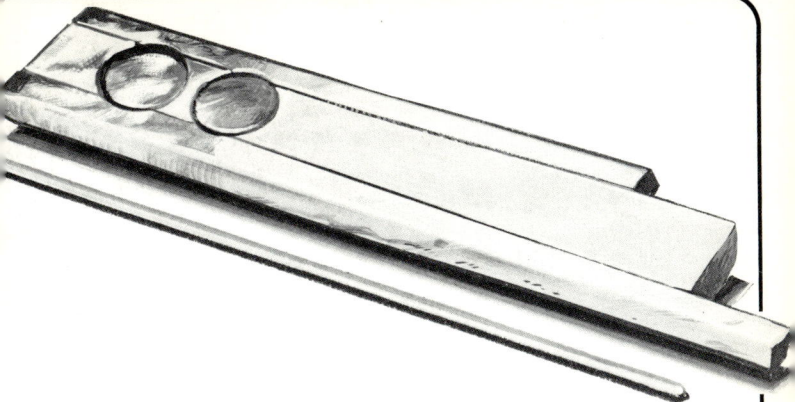

The Development of the Alphabet

In early scripts, a symbol stood for a sound. The sound could be one letter or a combination of letters. There were so many symbols that it was almost impossible to learn them all. Then a simpler, single-letter alphabet was developed.

Above: An Egyptian scribe used a thin board, or palette, like this. It holds brushes and solid cakes of red and black ink.

This diagram shows how some letters changed from Egyptian (1), to Ugaritic (2), Proto-Siniatic (3), South and North Semitic (4, 5), Hebrew (6), Archaic (7), Classical Greek (8), and Roman (9).

Meaning:	1	2	3	4
Water	ᚢᚢᚢ	⊱	ᚢᚢ	⊴
Fish	🐟	▼	🐟	⊓
Eye	👁	◁	👁	O

5	6	7	8	9
ᛉ	D	ᚢ	M	M
≢	D	I	Ξ	X
O	Y	O	O	O

Signs of Civilization—Money

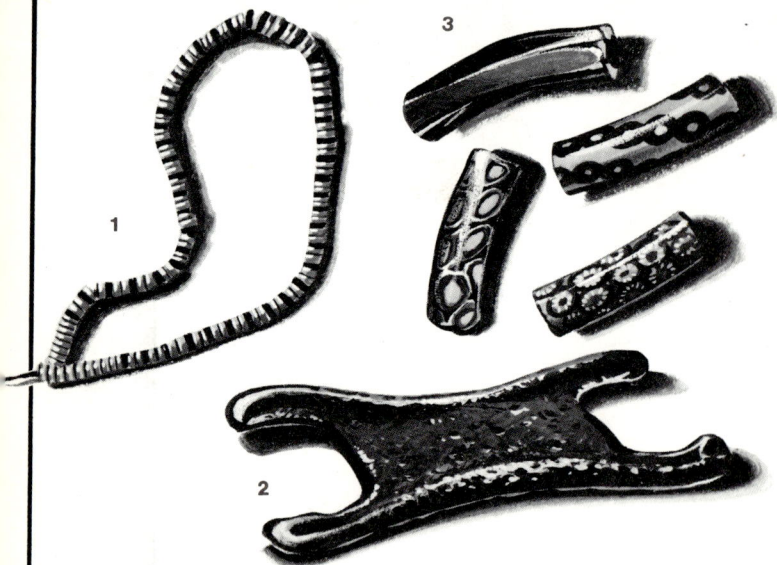

The need for trade goes back at least as far as the Stone Age. Every ancient society had some crop or material that another group needed. Farmers might have extra grain, but no wood for building huts. People living in rich forestland might have more timber than they could use. And so they traded.

For a long time, tribes and villages traded crops, crafts, stone, and other goods with one another. This system, called barter, did not always

work very well. Some objects being traded were not equal in value. When that happened, one trader would have to offer several items in exchange.

The next step was to find something—certain shells, for example—and figure the value of each item in shells. Traders could pay in equal goods—or in shells.

The Arrival of Money

Money, in the form of coins, was first used for payment and trade in Lydia in western Asia

Electrum coin
(actual size)

(1) A string of coconut and shell pieces used by South Sea islanders. (2) A Mycenaean "talent." (3) Beads from Africa. (4) Electrum coin. (5) A coin from Athens. (6) A Chinese coin of 600 BC.

Minor. The coins were made of electrum, a mixture of silver and gold. The idea was borrowed by the Greeks. Soon all the Mediterranean states were making their own money.

The Chinese, so far away, were not in touch with these lands. Yet at about the same time they also began to make and use coins.

Science and Archaeology

Archaeologists never stop looking for ways to learn about the past. And modern science can help. With thermoluminescence, scientists know the age of pottery. They can measure the amount of the element carbon 14 in an object. This, too, tells how old the object is. Counting a tree's rings gives its age—but archaeologists don't always find a handy tree!

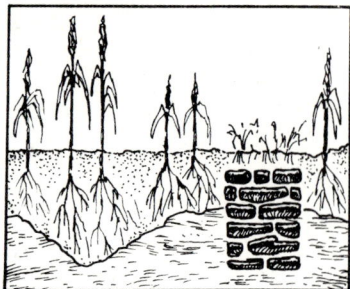

Sometimes, remains below the ground affect the plants above. Photographs taken from the air can show these changes. And then archaeologists know where to dig.

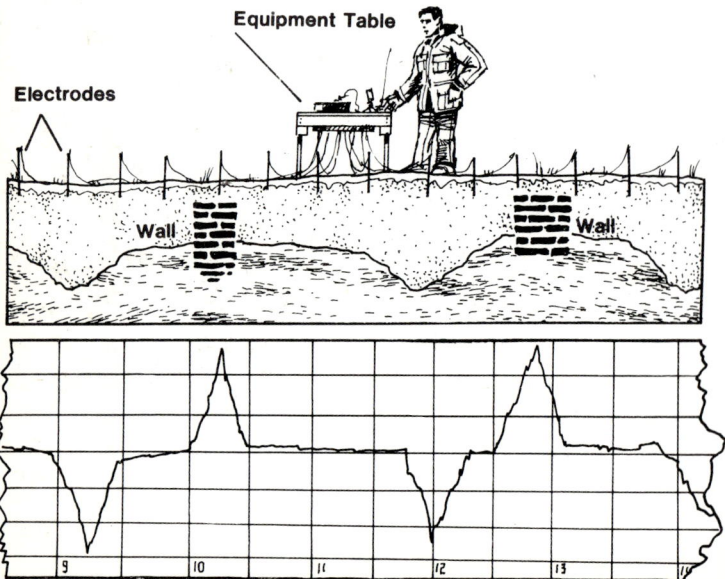

Equipment Table

Electrodes

Wall   Wall

To tell what is beneath the ground, scientists measure the moisture in the soil. They use special instruments called electrodes. The amount of water will be different if there is something underground.

Archaeologists even explore ruins under the sea. When studying a shipwreck, they divide the area into small squares. They examine every square. They don't want to miss a thing!

Buried in Ash

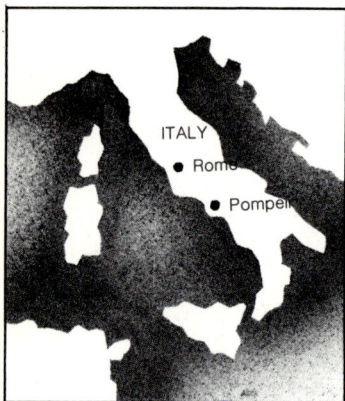

There are many reasons why some things have lasted since ancient times. Some of them were hidden, in tombs or beneath the ground. Some things were saved just by chance. And other objects, buildings, and even bodies lasted for another reason. Volcanoes and earthquakes buried whole towns and kept them preserved!

How a cast was made of a dog at Pompeii

This dog was buried in ash when Mount Vesuvius blew its top.

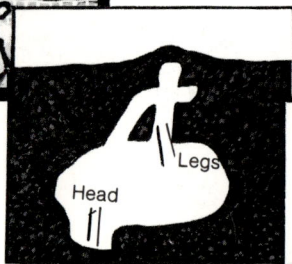

Over the years, the body rotted away. But its shape remained in the hard ash.

Archaeologists filled the shape with plaster. Then they chipped the ash away.

Pompeii and Herculaneum

In August of the year AD 79, Mount Vesuvius in Italy came alive. The ground shook and the sky rained fire. And the towns of Pompeii and Herculaneum disappeared. They were buried under piles of pumice and ash.

Roman writers told of the events of that terrible day. It was a tragedy for the people of the towns. But it was good luck for archaeologists. The pumice and ash preserved so much. Digging in the towns gives us a wonderful picture of what life was like so long ago.

Thera

Archaeologists are also digging in Thera (Santorin), an island north of Crete. There, too, a volcano destroyed an entire town and preserved it in ash.

Poisonous fumes killed this man before he could escape.

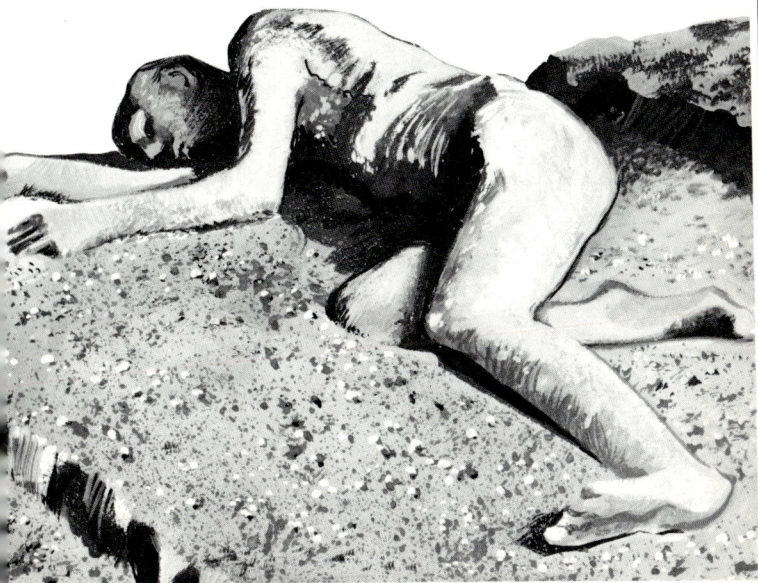

Treasure Trove

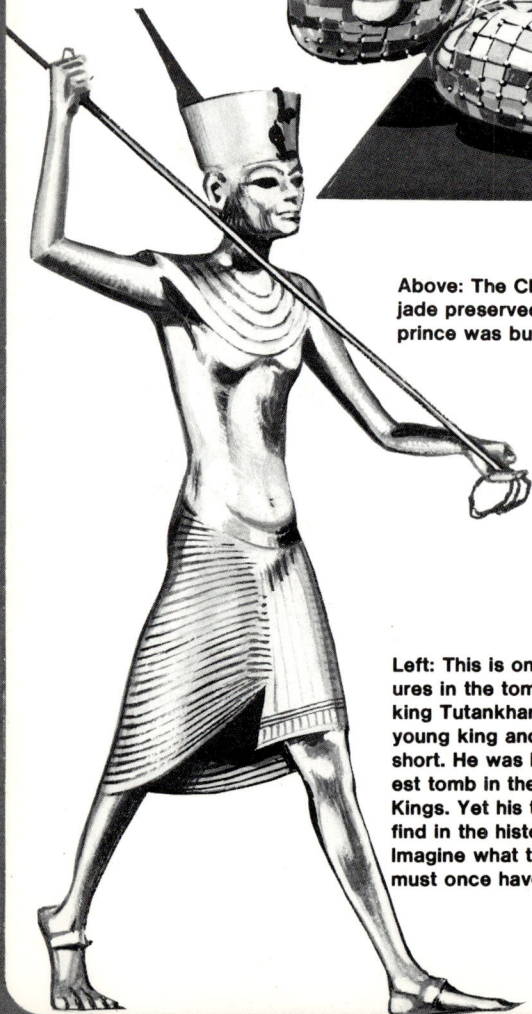

Above: The Chinese thought that jade preserved things. So this prince was buried in a suit of jade.

Left: This is one of many gold figures in the tomb of the Egyptian king Tutankhamen. He was a young king and his reign was short. He was buried in the smallest tomb in the Valley of the Kings. Yet his tomb is the richest find in the history of archaeology. Imagine what the larger tombs must once have held!

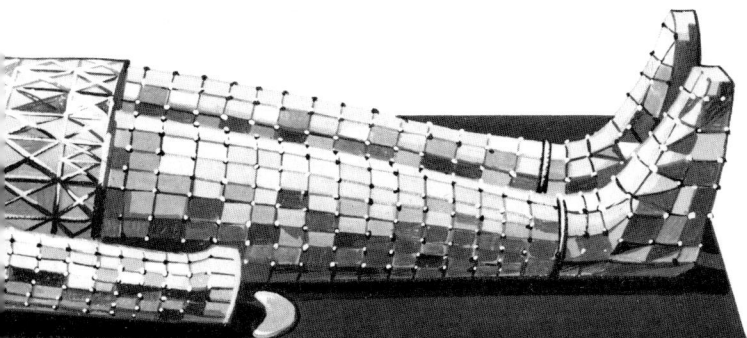

Many objects have lasted until modern times because they were thrown away. And of course some items were simply lost. Others may have been buried during times of trouble—and never found again. Some objects were buried in tombs with the dead. But grave robbers have stolen many riches from the tombs.

Most of the things that archaeologists find were the belongings of ordinary people. Once in a while, they uncover real treasure beneath the ground. But every object, no matter how small, is a special clue—a clue to the secrets of the ancient world.

Parts of the Puzzle

When you think about all the years that have gone by since early farmers were making pottery, hammering metal, carving wood, it is amazing that anything has lasted. And when archaeologists dig in the area of an ancient village or city, they do so with great care. Nothing, no matter how tiny, is lost. Every object is a piece of the puzzle that is our understanding of ancient times.

And so if you ever find an ancient object, don't move it. Call an expert. Just think—you may add to our understanding of ancient civilizations, of our world, and of ourselves.

Index